T0006262

HOW READY ARE YOU FOR LOVE?

The School of Life

Published in 2023 by The School of Life
930 High Road, London, N12 9RT
First published in the USA in 2023

Designed and typeset by Ryan Bartaby
Printed in China by Leo Paper Group

A proportion of this book has appeared online at:
theschooloflife.com/articles

The School of Life publishes a range of books on essential topics in
psychological and emotional life, including relationships, parenting,
friendship, careers and fulfilment. The aim is always to help us
to understand ourselves better – and thereby to grow calmer, less
confused and more purposeful. Discover our full range of titles,
including books for children, here: www.theschooloflife.com/books

The School of Life also offers a comprehensive therapy service,
which complements, and draws upon, our published works:
www.theschooloflife.com/therapy

www.theschooloflife.com

ISBN 978-1-915087-11-9

10 9 8 7 6 5 4 3 2 1

HOW READY

ARE YOU

FOR LOVE?

A path to more fulfilling
and joyful relationships

CONTENTS

I.

INTRODUCTION

The blame for most of what goes wrong in our love lives can be traced back to an almost innocent-sounding problem: a lack of self-knowledge. It is because we don't understand ourselves very well that we pick incompatible candidates, fail to assess our needs correctly, can't spot what we are doing to generate resentment and have trouble deciding whether to stay with or leave partners with whom we have run into difficulties.

Life normally ends up, at huge cost, eventually teaching us the necessary lessons. With the years, we tend to learn who we are, what makes us happy, what we do to frighten away those we like and how we sabotage our chances of contentment. By the time we reach retirement age, we may have correctly pieced together some good thoughts about how our early childhoods shaped our attachments; we may be getting better at apologising and saying important things directly. We may even accept that it is not – always and invariably – the other person's fault.

But the promise of this questionnaire is that, through a series of carefully structured enquiries, we may learn faster. Our deep minds will disclose themselves to us with greater ease and insight. We could – with luck – spare ourselves a few decades, and many crises too. The essays that accompany these questions are intended as conduits to self-reflection and prompts for emotional exploration; we might spend as much time reflecting as we do on reading. We are invited to recognise ourselves in certain doubtful or counterproductive patterns – and wince and vow to do things differently.

It may be best to answer the questions quickly. 'Not thinking too much' can help our true natures to manifest themselves more cleanly. Speed can help us to catch our defences unaware. The inside back flap of the book has space to record our answers. Once we have worked through the series, we can retrace our steps and – using the grading system at the back – add up our score, which is designed to give us a sense of our overall levels of emotional progress. We might then ask a prospective or actual partner to do the same, which could make for a valuable game on an early date.

As ever, we should not expect to be entirely mature in many areas: imperfection is the general rule; we are never done with 'growing up'. Love is a skill, not an emotion – and one we seldom receive systematic instruction in. However urgent our longing for love might be, a satisfying relationship only seems possible after we make considerable conscious effort to master the quirks of our obtuse minds. This book hopes to introduce us to some central unknown bits of ourselves – in the name of the love we long for.

II.

THE
QUESTIONNAIRE

1. Which of these sentences best captures for you the reality of dating nowadays?

---

a) There's an abundance of choice; no one needs to 'settle'.

---

b) It's always going to be a struggle to find a half-decent partner.

For most of human history, the dating game was stable and uneventful for a banal yet immovable reason: it was extremely hard to meet anyone acceptable – and everyone knew it. There were only limited numbers of people in the village, travel was expensive and social occasions were few and far between.

This created a lot of difficulties: it encouraged people to accept offers from suitors they were unconvinced by; it meant that lovers who would have delighted each other died lonely and unfulfilled because there were mountains or a few rivers between them.

Technology has flattened the obstacles and turned the world into an intimate living room. But this break-through at the level of introduction has obscured an ongoing challenge at the level of viability: we may all have become easier to meet, but we are not, perhaps, any easier to love. We remain – each one of us – highly challenging proposi-tions for anyone to take on: we are liable to be impatient and short-tempered, we make unjust accusations, we are rife with self-pity and we are not well practised at expressing our needs in a way that renders us comprehensible to others – just to start the list ...

That we can meet so many people has bred in us a charming yet ultimately tricky idea – which engulfs us any time we hit difficulties – that we are in trouble primarily be-cause we have not yet encountered 'the one'. The reason why there is friction and longing, we tell ourselves, has nothing to do with certain stubborn sides of our natures or with a range of paradoxes in the human condition as a whole; it is only a matter of needing to hunt further for a more reasonable candidate who will, at last, see things our way.

We are fortunate to be living in an era of immense choice, but this advantage will in the end have failed us if we allow it to distract us from the enduring requirement to nurture the understanding, forbearance and self-knowledge on which all realistic chances of successful love must ultimately rely.

2. The reason love has been difficult for me until now is:

---

a) I haven't yet met the right person.

---

b) I am far from perfect.

Dating apps may have made it infinitely easier to connect, but they haven't helped us to be one bit more patient, imaginative, forgiving or empathetic – that is, any more adept at the arts that render relationships viable. Most of the issues we experience with one candidate can be expected to show up, in comparable guises, with almost anyone we find.

The modern world is built on the promise of choice. But the thought that there is always someone better waiting in the wings for us has the power to drain us of the patience and modesty necessary to grapple with the tensions that are likely to come our way whomever we are with. We too easily forget that almost everyone is a charming prospect so long as we know nothing about them. Part of what it takes to be ready for love is to keep in mind the contortions of character that we cannot, as yet, know too much about: the bad moods that lurk behind the energetic smiles, the difficult pasts that lie beneath the lustrous eyes, the tangled psyches that reside beneath a stated love of straightforward pursuits like camping or cookery.

Once we have had a reasonable look around, the bulk of our efforts should not be directed towards trying to meet ever more people, but towards getting to the root of what makes it hard to live with any one candidate we might have found.

We will be ready for love when we surrender some of our excited sense of possibility and recognise that, though we might have many choices, we don't – in reality – have so many options. It may sound dark, but it may, in its own way, be a liberating realisation that can set us free to honour the full potential of all those we have already started to know.

3. How much hope do you
    have of finding 'the one'?

_____

a) There are some truly amazing
    people out there.

_____

b) Everyone is – from close
    up – humblingly difficult.

We tend to associate optimism with increased chances of success; we say that those who expect the best will be readiest to capitalise on the opportunities that come their way. But when it comes to relationships, a degree of strategic pessimism may in reality be the friend of a flourishing love life.

There is a particular kind of sickness that befalls us when we continually replenish our hopes of strangers and keep looking out for perfection. We gaze across restaurants or the aisles of trains and imagine that in the eyes of every enticing new person must lie degrees of sensitivity and gentleness, cleverness and depth that we have until now searched for in vain.

The intensity of our enthusiasm is touching, but it betrays a disloyalty towards certain unbudgeable facts of human nature. None of us has been spared substantial degrees of folly and meanness, arduousness and immaturity. However charming the exterior, the reality of life with anyone will include unavoidable amounts of anger, irritation and misunderstanding.

Such a conclusion, though bleak, can be a necessary base upon which to establish a willingness to keep going with one particular lover and acknowledge our own failings as partners.

We grow prepared for love when we start to come to terms with the perennially shocking and still somewhat unbelievable idea that perfect people do not exist.

4. What feels important in a prospective partner?

a) Beauty, sexiness, health, financial prowess, domestic skill, wit, sociability, optimism, vigour, curiosity, political compatibility, intellect, musical rhythm, cooking flair, patience, generosity and creativity.

b) Kindness, vulnerability and understanding.

Part of the difficulty of modern relationships stems from the complexity of what we are trying to do in them. We tend to seek an ideal partner who can blend the roles of lover, best friend, household manager, chauffeur, cook, kindergarten teacher, counsellor, financial advisor and sex therapist. We imbibe messages that love befitting of the name must involve the almost complete merger of two lives, united by relentless passion and flawless psychological mutuality. We have nothing but scorn for those who might contemplate 'compromise'.

Our romanticism sounds like a precondition of love, but it may in reality prove to be a particular enemy of meeting anyone; against such hopes, the only state that can guarantee us immunity from disappointment is singledom.

We can be liberated to love by a more restricted notion of what a fulfilling love story needs to achieve. It is by ordering and limiting our priorities that we secure the best chance of zeroing in on a worthy mate.

Three requirements for contentment stand out. Firstly, we need kindness: someone undamaged enough to have the energy to nurse the sufferings of those they are close to; someone who has been looked after for long enough to be able to care for others in turn. Secondly, we need someone with a capacity to be vulnerable, to have shed the temptations of defensiveness or aloofness; someone grown up enough not to mind admitting to their more dependent and tender sides. Thirdly, we require someone who will be excited to pursue a rational understanding of how relation-ships work, so that we and they can together overcome the inevitable obstacles and tensions of love through constant dialogue underpinned by curiosity and mental openness.

We can deal with most flaws so long as these three ingredients are in place, while any number of qualities may not satisfy us so long as they are not. We may be far less choosy than we fear once we grow more focused on what we actually need.

5. How prone are you
    to crushes?

_____

a) Very.

_____

b) I'm trying to get
    over the habit.

A strong propensity to form crushes on people has its endearing aspects; it suggests a touching level of responsiveness to others and an honesty about admitting to our hopes. As we wander the world in a crush-ready state, we swiftly imagine elevated degrees of accomplishment and desirability in every new person. We fall 'in love' at the supermarket and in the check-in queue, at the garden centre and at the bus stop, in the doctor's waiting room and at the computer repair shop.

The habit may seem innocent enough, but it suggests a fateful misunderstanding of psychology for which we may, in time, have to pay an extremely high price. We don't have to doubt that there are indeed people whose faces and surface manner imply all manner of enchanting qualities. But we begin to take our first steps towards emotional maturity when we finally accept (with deep sorrow) that, appearances notwithstanding, everyone is – ultimately – profoundly peculiar and, to put it in a colloquial way, mad: disturbed by their childhoods, unable to understand themselves, inclined to error and perversity and in complicated ways serious trouble to be around.

We don't need to know the specifics of anyone to understand this of everyone – and this background knowledge is what should inform, and dampen, our inclinations to latch onto a continuous roll call of strangers as possible solutions to our dreams.

We ready ourselves for the hard work of love by

accepting, with sorrow and wry amusement, that the question should never be whether or not a potential partner is deranged or difficult to be around. We can take such dark eventualities for granted and should instead simply settle on swiftly finding out the particular nuances of their follies in order to ascertain whether we can bear them – and they can bear ours.

6. How long could you stand to be single?

a) A year or so. Maybe two.

b) Forever, if I have to be.

It is an irony of love that we are best able to choose a partner when we are most able to do without one. It's the sense that we cannot get through the weeks without someone to comfort us, without a special person in whom we can invest our energies, that leads us to respond incautiously to the prospects before us. The more we cannot do without romantic love, the greater the risk that we will be hurt in its pursuit.

The best way to prepare for love is therefore to develop a host of coping strategies for its absence. We need, first and foremost, friends who will bring to companionship some of the same intimacy and supportiveness that our societies (wrongly) teach us to associate exclusively with sexual relationships. We need someone who can come round when we are tearful and ill, someone in whom we can confide the extent of our self-doubts and confusions – and around whom there will be no need to imply that we are either normal or well. We need, too, distractions, journeys, favourite cafés, very elderly and very young acquaintances, political interests, artistic curiosities, household chores, ideally a small garden or a flower box – and, of course, an imaginatively stocked library.

To be desperate for love means being susceptible to choosing anyone over favouring someone in particular. We will be ready to pick intelligently when we have learnt to be entirely and justly unfrightened of our own company.

7. If I asked someone on a date and they said 'no', it would be a sign that:

_____

a) I didn't deserve to exist.

_____

b) They were perhaps busy, not single or – understandably enough – interested in another type of person.

Our capacity to withstand the rebuffs and jostling of the dating game relies on what we are able to hear when the word 'no' is mentioned. For those of us most at risk of giving up on the opportunities and joys of love, it is never just a 'no'; it is confirmation of something that we have suspected about ourselves all along: that we are essentially hideous, deformed, diseased, a menace and an object of pity and derision. The person who has rebuffed us may not (we concede) specifically have said quite this to us, but we are sure enough that this is what was meant. And this is why we will take to our bed for days and never venture anything as foolish as an invitation ever again.

We loosen our hold on our susceptibility when we recognise that it is likely to have had a long history. We feel unlovable now because we have – probably – felt somewhat unlovable from the start. We didn't benefit from the sort of childhood that would have afforded us a sense of our fundamental worthiness and right to exist, and that is why every rejection has the power to catapult us back to a state of primal, unacknowledged despair.

Liberation awaits us when we are able to separate out present friction from early tragedy. The people we attempt to ask out for dinner are not – in reality – the figures from yesterday on whom we depended and who let us down when we had few other options. We don't need to take their verdict as anything other than a straightforward declaration of unavailability from which we need to draw no grand conclusions as to our significance as human beings. We will scatter our invitations as widely and as innocently as we must when we grow able to accept that sometimes a 'no' may just be a 'no'.

8. Someone you have liked for many months without knowing whether or not they liked you back becomes extremely sweet and warm. Are you inclined to:

---

a) Suddenly wonder what might be wrong with them and go a bit cold?

---

b) Feel grateful and love them back with enthusiasm?

One of the greatest challenges of love lies in how we can respond to the moment we ostensibly all long for: the moment of reciprocation. However much we thought we wanted someone, the realisation that they want us too can catapult us into a peculiar state of ingratitude and irritation.

In the wake of a declaration of affection, our beloved, in whom we erstwhile so fervently believed, may suddenly strike us as banal, unoriginal and burdensome. Of course, they have not – in reality – become objectionable; the problem lies in how we feel about ourselves. The more we are unconvinced of our own lovability, the more we will be pulled towards denigrating anyone with the poor judgement to approve of someone like us. Why would anyone decent think any better of us than we – deep down – think of ourselves?

At the same time, the greater will be our propensity to be drawn to people whom we are unconsciously sure will remain distant, unavailable and subtly uninterested in genuine connection. Such characters will maintain a mesmeric hold on us not because they are deserving of our love, but because their dismissal of us accords so perfectly with our underlying sense of our own value. They hate us as much as we hate ourselves.

If we find ourselves repeatedly cooling on anyone the instant they evince signs of mutual interest, we should reroute our suspicions back on ourselves. We should not question our admirer so much as question why we have ended up so critical of anyone who might evaluate us tenderly. Our disgust with kindly and enthusiastic partners is our self-hatred returning to us in disguised form. We are punishing anyone who cannot match our elevated degrees of self-contempt.

Our kindly lover may not be any sort of fool; they may have just guessed something about us that we still have to work on accepting about ourselves: that we are worthy of ample kindness and respect.

9. A hugely charming dinner date mentions in an offhand way that they're 'not so interested in introspection'. Do you:

a) Smile benignly and move on?

b) Finish the course swiftly and engineer an exit without dessert?

It can take a while before we grow properly attuned to what we should run away from in love. The real dangers lie not so much in administrative or social failings: a lack of punctuality, a habit of leaving the fridge door slightly open, a shyness in public, hard-going friends ... The danger lies in resistance to the single most important indicator of successful long-term unions: a capacity for introspection.

Someone who cannot reflect on their actions, who grows defensive when their attention is brought to bear on their responses to situations, who cannot explore the link between their present and their early years and who refuses to trace their moods of irritability and sullen detachment back to their actual causes is likely to be responsible for increasing friction and eventual disenchantment.

An ability to apologise, to soften initial responses and to view things through other lenses requires that we be willing to wander in an unfrightened way through the corridors of our minds. Those who cannot sit with their own thoughts won't be able to display the emotional tact or forbearance required to cope with the turmoil of the average relationship.

We should forgive many failings, but we should be rightfully impatient with, and frightened of, those who – halfway through an initial meal – nakedly scorn the project of self-knowledge. We should beware of people who might have extreme objections to finishing a questionnaire like this.

10. Early in a relationship, a companion, kindly and with obvious good will, asks, 'And how are you mad?' Do you:

a) Take offence?

b) Calmly take them through some of the issues that you suffer from?

We would, naturally, all love to be sane – and, in our more naïve moments, we assume we might be so. But wisdom begins when we can recognise the more complicated truth that no one reaches adulthood without suffering from a significant degree of emotional impairment. Even if our parents didn't do anything especially wrong and without any sharply defined traumas behind us, we are likely to be less than entirely balanced and distinctly inclined to over- or under-react to the world around us.

The saner among us are sufficiently self-aware not, on top of everything else, to insist on their own normalcy and flawless mental health. They have the maturity to accept their immaturities; they have the wisdom to have a map of their unbudgeable follies to hand – and to be able to lend it occasionally to those who have taken on the task of living alongside them.

We don't fortunately need those we love to be sane (or we would be forever alone). We merely need them to be able – in their calmer moments – to admit to their strangeness with a degree of grace and good humour. They would ideally be able to tell us, before they have hurt us too badly, some of what is likely to be most difficult about living close to them. They will warn us about their bad moods after work, their awkwardness around their mother or their tendency to panic at airports.

Their confessions won't magically remove every problem, but they will hugely attenuate their impact. We are infinitely more likely to forgive someone who has a good sense

of what they need to be forgiven for than someone who main-
tains their innocence against all odds.

It should never be taken as an insult to be asked how
we are mad. It merely means that someone else is interested
enough to find out the specific ways in which we partake in the
universal tendency towards oddity and difficulty. We should be
ready with the sort of answer that can reassure someone that,
though we will at points be tricky to live with, we will never
add self-righteousness and defensiveness to our list of flaws.

11. **Are you easy to live with?**

a) Yes, fairly.

b) Of course not.

One of the difficulties of spending too long on our own is that we can start to believe that we are easy to live with – if only we had someone who wanted to try to do so. The single state strips us of opportunities for those more bracing moments of self-knowledge that commonly arise in couples' lives, when we recognise new varieties of delusion, self-pity or obnoxiousness.

When we are on our own, not wishing to offend or alienate us, our parents will probably steer clear of telling us any difficult truths. Our friends mostly don't care enough about us to say anything – they want the odd pleasant evening with us, not to reform our natures. We might at times dimly remember some acute comments that an ex-partner made about our characters before they left us, but it is only too easy to put this down to meanness. Most of our exes simply said they needed 'more space'.

When we are the only person we see every morning and evening, our minds naturally edit out from memory our worst periods of moodiness, despair and irrationality; we simply don't remember that we spent most of one weekend ruminating over an instance of wounded pride or looking up peculiar things on the internet. We don't notice how stubborn and unfair we can be when there is no one on whom to exercise our flaws. We can't see how weird we are about the contents of the fridge and the right way to say certain words.

As a result, we may enter relationships with a blithe confidence that we are a simple proposition for another person. It isn't that we have nothing pleasant at all to bring to them, but we omit to appreciate just how many difficulties we will also inevitably entangle them in, given the oddities in our nature.

The easiest people to live with turn out to be those with the keenest awareness that they might not be any such thing.

12. A partner starts to tease you with kindness about a few of your eccentricities. Do you:

---

a) Wonder why they don't love you anymore?

---

b) Enjoy their wry take on your flaws?

There is a sort of teasing that meanly picks away at a tender part of our nature and makes us recoil in hurt, but there is another kind that can be strangely pleasant to be on the receiving end of. All of us recognise, in our honest and courageous moments, that we incline in certain areas towards irrationality and imbalance. The good teaser is someone who has observed us with kindness and intelligence and, motivated by a desire to educate rather than humiliate us, deftly points out a few areas in which we appear to have left reason or good manners behind. When we laugh, it's a sign that we have understood the critique, that we have acknowledged areas of absurdity and are in the background pleased that someone cares about us enough to bother with our education.

The good teaser lets us know with sensitivity that we have been talking a little too much about ourselves, that it has been a long time since we invested in any new clothes, that our political opinions are on the wrong edge of strident or that we are at risk of overdoing gloom or cheerfulness. A good teaser brings us back into line with maximal delicacy; their work constitutes a delicate and civilised attempt to teach us how to be better people.

We all, at some level, want to be loved 'for who we really are'. But nothing more unfruitful could be imagined, given how much we need to develop into someone we aren't as yet. It may give us a rush of pleasure to be told that we are already perfect, but it is a great deal more satisfying (and reassuring) to be seen for our flaws and playfully encouraged on a path to greater virtue. The good teaser helps us to know that we can be loved both for who we are now and, even more so, for who we might one day become.

13. **What do you need to be teased for?**

a) Why are you asking?

b) It's a long list.

It's a sign of emotional maturity to be able to summon up an extensive range of areas in which we suspect we are probably – to a greater or lesser extent – foolish and flawed. We should know that we deserve, and need, to be teased.

We will almost certainly not be able to laugh at ourselves very much of the time if left to our own devices. We incline naturally towards undue seriousness and self-justification. But we should hope to build up enough of an external perspective on ourselves to know – at least in general form – where our buried ridiculousness lies. We should – with a wince – be able to admit that there is something odd about the way we relate to our appearance, or that there is something regrettable about our attitude to art, friendship or ambition. We should realise that we really do need to laugh about our habits in the kitchen or the way we behave on holiday.

It's common to hope for a partner with a 'good sense of humour'. What we are in essence looking for is not comedy in general, but – very wisely – that most essential ingredient of workable relationships: a capacity to laugh heartily at our own excesses.

Mature lovers should have an ever-expanding list somewhere to hand with the helpful title: Things I Need to Be Teased For. It would be interchangeable with a list we might otherwise title: Areas in Which I Know I Am Slightly Awful.

14. Someone keeps falling in love with unavailable people. What might be the problem?

a) They are just unlucky.

b) It's worth asking them how they get on with their mother or father.

Psychotherapy has made a momentous claim that we might heartily wish was in no way true: that the way we love as adults is to a conclusive extent determined by our early relationship with the parent whose gender we are attracted to. We are engaged – in a way we can rarely see too well – in patterns of repetition in love.

Sometimes, these patterns are pleasant. We were loved with generosity and sympathy; now we look for such virtues in our own relationships. But more commonly, the repetition goes in a darker direction.

Our father was a withholding, silent, domineering sort; now we push away kindly men and head for those who will leave us feeling belittled and inadequate. Our mother was emotionally cold and vain; now we are sickened by women who are even-tempered and affectionate, while feeling mysteriously drawn to characters who are unreliable and sadistic.

This process tends to operate in insidious ways. Our father might have worked in finance, so we try to avoid all men in business. But then we discover that the poet or primary school teacher with whom we have built a life eerily shares, at a psychological level, many of the traits that our father once had. Our mother might have been obviously glamorous and theatrical, but that seems not to ensure that the more modestly dressed landscape gardener we have chosen won't – in terms of our relationship with her – repeat most of the varieties of emotional alienation that we knew so well in childhood.

We are too easily trapped within a web spun by Mum or Dad before we were 10. No wonder many of us despise psychotherapy as much as we respect it.

15. If you had a bad relationship with the parent whose gender you are attracted to, what might you do to mitigate the possible effects?

a) Nothing in particular. This sounds like psychobabble.

b) Three times a week of therapy, a lot of reading and immense vigilance.

Our ability to avert disaster is fragile at the best of times. Nevertheless, knowing that we might be in grave danger can, with a fair wind, help us to avert some of the more obvious catastrophes we might be headed for.

If we were to realise the perilous situation we were in on account of our childhoods, we might exercise extreme vigilance around people we were instinctively attracted to. We might assume that almost anyone we felt mysteriously and powerfully drawn to would probably turn out to be wrong. We might learn to resist falling in love at first sight – and would be just as careful about swiftly falling into hatred (our habit of dismissing otherwise kindly people as 'boring' or 'unattractive' could be as suspicious as our proclivity to develop crushes). We would understand that we needed to fight our instincts at every turn, because of how badly our pasts have corrupted them.

We would wonder whether the most innocent-seeming candidate might, after all, where it counted, be just like our mother or father – despite sharing none of their outward traits. We would become skilfully paranoid about our judgement.

Keeping all this in mind, it might take us a bit longer to reach the altar – but so long as we had done our work, when we finally did so, we might plausibly trust that we were not, after all, stepping into the future in the company of a secret version of Mum or Dad.

16. You are in a mood in which you deeply need to hear reassurance that your partner still cares about you. Which of these are you most likely to do?

---

a) Bury yourself in your work – or a good book.

---

b) Ask them for reassurance.

We are used to hearing how hard it can be to tell a partner that we love and need them at the start of a relationship. Unfortunately, the need for reassurance – to hear that we are cherished and important in another's life – never quite goes away.

It's a symptom of a particular form of emotional maturity (which our childhoods gift us – or do not) to be able to admit that, despite our adult competence in many areas, there are times when we want nothing more than to curl up in a ball and be indulged as if we were a small child or a puppy; moments when we passionately seek a demonstration that we matter and want our partner to call us by our favourite nickname and soothe our brow.

The difficulty comes in how we handle the fear of rejection that accompanies this quest for reassurance. For some of us, the fear is so great, the apprehension that our partner will not come through so pervasive, that we opt to say nothing at all. In fact, we may do everything to imply that we are entirely fine on our own, at precisely the moment when we long intensely for a cuddle – so as to avoid an intolerable encounter with our own vulnerability. We pretend that we have to see a friend, finish some work or make a solo trip to another country. It feels too dangerous to take our partner into the extent of our need for their tenderness.

If we lacked a secure impression of being loved as a child, our hunger for love in adulthood can drive us towards a paradoxical pattern whereby we display only extreme independence, which masks an unreconciled attitude to weakness.

It is a serious achievement of maturity to be able to own up to a latent wish that our partner will tell us – perhaps not for the first time today – that they do still very much care about us.

17. You feel a sense of distance has somehow crept in between you and your partner, which you can't quite explain or account for. It's both minor and yet niggles at you. How might you respond?

---

a) Get annoyed with them about something practical and procedural they might have done wrong.

---

b) Explain the pain you are in and reveal how much of it stems from love – and a fear of its loss.

A tempting response, when we feel at risk of being sidelined or ignored by a partner, is to pick a fight with them. At precisely the moment when we want to be comforted and gain renewed evidence of their affection, we identify one of their flaws and come down hard on it. We remember that they have (again) failed to repair the front door, that they have forgotten to make a doctor's appointment, that they were silent and uninspiring with a friend of ours or that their shoes or hair are in a shameful state.

Our aggression embodies an attempt to redress a balance of power that feels appallingly in their favour. We choose to escape our reliance on them through an exaggerated show of anger and blame. We come across as fierce, independent, chiding and akin to a withholding and punitive parent (the very sort that might once have made our life hell).

The irony is how entirely contrary our real intentions are. 'Find yourself someone else to pick up your dirty laundry' really means 'Please promise you're never going to leave me.' 'Don't think I am going to put up with your nonsense forever' masks a searing feeling that 'I couldn't live without you.'

It is a marker of exceptional emotional wherewithal to be able to express longing and a wish for comfort without giving way to those far more tempting and robust alternatives: anger and blame.

18. Your partner has a habit of being unusually warm when they meet attractive, successful strangers at parties. How might you respond to this habit?

---

a) Silence. Why give them a victory by displaying your annoyance?

---

b) Tell them – with calm, sincerity and wit – that you are a jealous sort.

To love someone is to give them a potentially appalling degree of control over our moods and well-being. With a glance or two in a certain direction, they have the power to unbalance us. They can make us doubt the very foundations of our lives simply by being animated for a few moments at a party around someone who appears more beautiful and successful than we are.

Unfortunately, it isn't easy to reveal how small and bereft they can make us feel. We are surrounded by messages that tell us that being grown up must involve strength and a refusal to remain at anyone's mercy.

We may therefore respond to twinges of jealousy with attempts at ruthless denial. Why would we give our lover a further victory by revealing how much they are able to unsettle us?

As ever, though, we do not need to apologise or wish away our less robust sides: we should strive to reveal them frankly, with confidence that they belong to every human, however evolved, and perhaps couch our extreme sensitivity in a small joke at our own expense.

'If you carry on being so charming to them, I may just have to make my apologies and throw myself off the balcony. You would understand. As I've always told you, I'm the jealous sort. I would so appreciate it, though, if you didn't invite them to the funeral.'

We recover a measure of mastery over our (highly understandable) jealousy not by pretending that it doesn't exist, but by making no bones as to its overwhelming power. To hear a claim that someone is 'never jealous' should always make us wonder why and how their true needs might have grown so inadmissible to them.

19. Your partner asks you whether something is wrong. Something actually is – deep inside, you're annoyed with something they have done or said. How might you respond?

a) By saying, 'Nothing' and turning away.

b) By finding a way – hard though it is – to tell them what is wrong.

Few things mar greater stretches of our emotional lives than the poignant and complex form of response to emotional injury that we know as sulking.

Sulking is – from the outside – a highly paradoxical pattern of behaviour. A partner has in some way offended us. They have told a story in public that we wanted them to keep private, they have shown us a lack of tact, they have forgotten an important occasion, they have failed to listen to us.

We want them so deeply to understand us – and rescue us from loneliness and inattention. And yet the sulker acts as if from an unhelpfully romantic hope: that another person should interpret them without them having spoken up about their needs. They dream that someone who truly loved them would know what they were upset about without requiring the offence to be spelt out to them in a medium as clumsy and as slow as language. They want to be understood without words.

Anyone who fails to do this is quickly taken by the sulker to be badly intentioned. There is little space to believe in innocent failures of empathy. The partner hasn't merely failed to grasp what is going on; their failure is willed, they are doing this on purpose. They are deliberately mocking us by making it seem as if they have no clue that it is our anniversary or that they have let out one of our secrets. To a feeling of abandonment, the sulker adds a layer of persecution.

For the sulker, it is a great deal more tempting to devote six hours to answering curtly, insisting that nothing is wrong and affecting a pained and melancholy look than to strive to delineate the nature of their hurt.

We are taking our first steps towards a less fraught kind of coupledom when we are finally able to tell someone who has upset us that they have upset us – preferably within the very half hour in which they have done so.

20. You have prepared your partner dinner. They compliment you kindly but mention that the pasta was, perhaps, a bit overcooked. How do you respond?

a) With a sense of hurt. How dare they!

b) Consider that it might be an idea to take the penne out a bit earlier next time.

The messages may be diverse: the pasta is a little overcooked. Or: it might be important to spend a bit more time on work. Or: perhaps you shouldn't speak so loudly to your mother in public.

These messages might be sincere and limited in their scope, but for a mind frayed by difficult early experiences, the true import of what is being said will stretch far beyond the objective surface declarations. This isn't an issue-specific commentary; it's an attack on the foundations of one's being.

For those who are susceptible, feedback has the power swiftly to evoke a more fundamental critique. What we actually hear is not that our cooking might benefit from a tweak (or that we might change the second paragraph or the colour of our pullover), but, surprisingly though devastatingly, that we do not deserve to exist, let alone expect any sympathy for our mishaps. Every evaluation that does not wholly support us feels close to a direct attempt to shut us down.

We have grown so defended because, at an age when we were excessively vulnerable, we may have suffered from an unendurable level of criticism that now renders us unable to stay steady in the face of feedback, however minor, about things we have done or said. We are perfectionists because there was never any option to be that far more realistic and tolerable thing: 'good enough'.

We will have made progress when we have learnt to trust that we may mess up supper (or substantial bits of our lives) – and yet remain adored and worthy.

21. Complete the following sentence without thinking too much. When two lovers get together, what tends to happen is:

_____

a) Pain and trouble.

_____

b) Tenderness.

The usefulness of 'not thinking too much' when we are asked to finish certain sentences is that the discipline can reveal, better than when we are given ample time, what we really think. Our true opinions can surge out of us with greater clarity when we don't have an opportunity to wonder what might sound normal or reasonable (and censor ourselves accordingly) – and instead let our gut dictate what we say.

What such exercises can release is the template that we carry within us about what relationships tend to be like and what is liable to happen as they unfold. These templates are built up in us over long years, most of them in childhood, as we extrapolate from our own stories and from the behaviours of those around us. Our impression of what might happen owes more than we rationally imagine to the scenes that we were exposed to in our young years and our experiences at the hands of those entrusted with our care.

The templates are then applied – with a speed and power we find it almost impossible to detect without help – to the relationships we get involved in as adults. The process is far from neutral in its impact. Our sense of what might happen tends to determine what will happen: a strong sense that most love stories end in acrimony or that most partners can't be trusted skews what we say, do and conclude as we advance through any actual relationship.

Before we ask someone to love us, we and they deserve to get a clearer map of the territory we imagine we will be in. We need to know what we think happens to lovers in general. Those who expect disaster tend to find it, or have a good shot at trying to create it.

22. Finish the following two sentences:

- *Most men are ...*
- *Most women are ...*

Were your answers:

---

a) Broadly negative?

---

b) Broadly positive?

Psychotherapy has been imaginative in alerting us to the phenomenon known as projection: the habit of applying expectations formed in childhood to the varied situations of adulthood. Becoming aware of our projections can be releasing because so many of them are unfair. Drawn from the limited experience of a child within a restricted family setting, they rarely do justice to reality. They universalise and apply to all partners a person encounters as an adult the cruel lessons of childhood – at the expense of a more nuanced and hopeful analysis of human nature.

Dad was mean; now all men are taken to be so.

Mum couldn't be trusted; now all women fall under a cloud of suspicion.

A partner may strive to reassure us and convince us of their fundamental benevolence, but when we are burdened with negative projections, they may flounder against our historically accumulated suspicions. We don't mean to be nasty; it is simply that our early role models can exert an undue and potentially decisive influence on how we perceive any later attachment figure.

The only way to defuse the power of projections is to become more aware of their presence – and then to develop into better historians of their formation. Knowing that we semiconsciously harbour anger, fear or cynicism towards the gender we are attracted to can liberate us to examine our judgements and drain them of misplaced pessimism or paranoia.

We aren't responsible for our past, but we do have a strong duty to cease looking at the present through its potentially cruelly distorted – and distorting – lenses.

23. You're in a relationship and your partner forgets your birthday. How might you be inclined to respond?

a) Say nothing and hope they realise eventually; it doesn't matter so much anyway. They may be very busy.

b) Point out that you like it when people make a bit of a fuss of you now and then; it makes you feel special.

One of the greatest sources of difficulty in relationships stems – paradoxically – from the strength of a person's wish not to be 'difficult'.

At first glance, a partner with an inclination to be 'easy' can feel like an advantage. They won't make a fuss about small things; they won't get obviously angry when you forget to mark an important date.

But the problem stems from the hidden cost that maintaining this outward equilibrium demands. No one is, in the end, genuinely and sincerely 'easy' in intimate relationships: everyone in love gets upset by so-called small things; it is inevitable when so much of our happiness is on the line. So, while we may well be bothered by difficulties thrown up by a lover, we should be even more worried by the total absence of friction. It's an indication that we are not as intimate as we should be – and that a reckoning is on the cards eventually, in some form or other.

It is the curse of certain people to have been brought up feeling an imperative never to cause problems for others. Maybe a mother was prone to rage and had to be appeased at every turn; perhaps a father was depressed and it felt too risky to show him anything but politeness. And so we ended up being a 'good child', always well behaved, always smiling, never a cause of tension, not because we were good all the way through – no one is or should be – but because the price of authenticity was too high.

As a result, one reaches adulthood with a powerful sense that our true self cannot be shown or accepted, even in close relationships; we smile a lot and take care never to be a bother. But the effort to suppress our discomforts will always backfire with devastating results down the line. Rather than shutting down feelings, it would be better if we could reveal them cleanly and quickly, even at the cost of a burst of rage and a ruined evening or two.

The effective way to please people is not to people-please, but to take the risk of behaving in a real way around them, which might well involve a few tantrums – something we should ultimately always be reassured by and feel grateful to be on the receiving end of.

24. Your partner makes moves that you know imply they would like to make love. On this occasion, though, you are not in the mood. What do you do?

---

a) Go along with it to be nice – these things matter.

---

b) Make efforts to explain that you love them but don't want to make love on this occasion.

The desire to people-please can reach a particularly acute pitch around love-making. We sense – not unfairly – that the desire for sex generally stems from a deep and vulnerable place and that rejection here will hurt more than in most areas. There are therefore outsize inducements to pretend that we are always in the mood and to smile – and to feign signs of deep enjoyment.

The problem is that the ultimate goal of love-making is not love-making so much as a sense of closeness. And the difficulty with sex that has been entered into for the sake of the partner's feelings is that it generates the very opposite of closeness: indeed, it traps us within the lonely cage of politeness.

The alternative way to be close without having sex comes from daring to explain – with deftness, sincerity and self-deprecating wit – why we don't want to have sex. It means feeling close enough with someone in order to take them through the ways we happen to be tired, disgruntled, sad or in a puritanical state of mind. Rather than an orgasm, the prize of such an approach is connection.

Being 'good in bed' is a rightfully esteemed quality, but we are apt to misunderstand what the feat actually involves when we picture it in aerobic terms. Good love-making doesn't in the end have anything directly to do with how we physically make love. It has to do with how honest and intimate we can be around love-making – something that must at points include a wish not to make love at all.

25. One member of a couple is finding it hard to desire their partner sexually. What might be the reason?

---

a) A lack of horniness.

---

b) A lack of trust.

It can be easy to misunderstand the roots of sexual excitement. We tend to focus overly on the externals: a certain sort of room, particular kinds of clothes, a certain level of hormones ... But the most important ingredient in encouraging us to take off our clothes and present ourselves without inhibition or fear is – in the end – trust. Trust that a partner has our best interests at heart, that we aren't ever going to be mocked, that there is loyalty and long-term concern at play, that we are with someone who can be delicate with our feelings. Sex itself may be rough and powerful; the feelings behind sex must be anything but.

This helps to explain why, after many years together, sex so often dies. The reasons tend to be brushed away as an inevitable feature of time. But while a long period in one another's company can on its own increase the risks of sexlessness, this is rarely what is at play. A lack of sex tends to be a symptom of hurt and anger – in other words, of broken trust. The reason why we're not in the mood seldom has anything to do with a lack of 'horniness'; it is because our deep selves remember that – three days before – our partner was less than courteous with us in public, or they haven't been listening to our concerns over the past months, or they seem distant and unfocused whenever we bring up a topic that matters to us.

We're apt not to realise the impact of small instances of neglect on our capacities to desire someone. We may not be aware that we are, in a quiet way, furious with our partner for making us feel invisible and therefore cannot abide them touching us. We aren't being mean; we're simply (silently) very hurt, but without the self-possession to know that we are so, let alone the courage to announce the problem cleanly.

This suggests that one of the best ways to ensure an active sex life isn't silk gowns or candles, but a forum in which resentments and points of tension can be aired and resolved. Sex begins long before sex is even a consideration.

26. You are in a relationship with someone you deeply love, but you notice yourself occasionally admiring other people in public places. How might you respond?

---

a) Feel guilty and furtive. Privately doubt if you're a good person.

---

b) Accept fleeting desires as a natural part of being alive; perhaps even mention them to your partner in a kind and unthreatening way.

The problem with our romantic view of sex is that it is in danger of forcing human nature into a shape it cannot realistically have – and of thereby contorting our spirits unbearably.

We tell ourselves that to love someone properly means foregoing all desires for any other member of our species until the day we die. The slightest stray thought, the most minor vagabond desire, any sexual fantasy in which the partner does not feature – all are framed as grounds for deep offence and evidence that our relationship will not last the course.

We are thereby doing our sincere feelings a grave injustice – and burdening ourselves with a guilt we don't deserve. There is no incompatibility whatsoever between a major commitment to one person and recurring sensations of desire for strangers. We should not expect lovers to overcome a normal part of the functioning of the mammalian mind in the name of an unholy ideal of purity.

Our love will become calmer and easier the more we focus on the genuine dangers to love that stem from emotional disconnection – and in the meantime take the quirks of sexuality into our stride. We shouldn't be reassured, either, when a partner insists that they have no interest whatsoever in any other human on earth. We should wonder what they are opting not to tell us about and why – and feel sad that we haven't as yet established a sufficient atmosphere of trust for the beautiful peculiarities of the sexual mind to be safely explored.

27. In bed, with a new partner, there's a kink you'd like to share; it might involve ropes, or power, or certain unusually frank words being said in a very particular way. What might you do?

---

a) Say little – these things feel personal for a reason.

---

b) Let out a hint, and ask what their kink might be.

Long before we were interested in sex, we will have received – in childhood – a sense of how legitimate and acceptable our desires and thoughts were. We might have been blamed (directly or covertly) for being a 'dirty little boy' or a 'naughty little girl'. Or, if we were lucky, the dramas and messes of childhood might have been accepted as entirely natural and a healthy part of development.

From such experiences, an inner conscience will have been formed in either a punitive or an indulgent direction. Many years later, in bed with a lover, it is this conscience that will determine how much of our reality we feel able to share with someone we care for.

Those who have made peace with their conscience will have a distinctive understanding of a much-contested word: 'normality'. They will have faith that all sorts of things are fundamentally normal even if they aren't spoken about so much in company. It might be normal to want to be flogged or to flog, to submit or to dominate, to insult or to coddle. It might be normal to be turned on by stray items of clothing: a particular kind of skirt or glove, hat or T-shirt. Sexuality may not follow ordinary logic, but it is not beyond understanding or sympathy.

The lover with an easy conscience can dare to let someone else in on their imagination, without excessive fear of judgement or rejection. The benefit stretches beyond an eventual mutual sex game. A partner may not even want what we want: what matters is that we have been able to risk showing them a byway of our deep self; the real benefit lies in closeness.

Anyone can be polite and good. The valuable achievement is to learn how to be different, authentic and 'bad' – that is, to allow ourselves to be known.

28. Why does sex matter?

a) It's evidence of desire.

b) It's evidence of closeness.

There is broad agreement on the centrality of sex within re-lationships. A couple who have a lot of sex are swiftly and intuitively understood to be in a good place; one where sex is rare or nonexistent cannot be expected to last the course.

Yet because these assumptions can seem so obvious, we're apt to grow confused about what precisely might be wrong with a couple where sex has stopped. It might not, ultimately, be a lack of sex that really counts – a thought that opens up new avenues of hope as well as concern when thinking about couples who rarely make love.

The advantage of sex is that it cannot occur without a high degree of vulnerability on both sides. The physical act requires an almost unavoidable degree of physical and emo-tional intimacy – which explains why sex can be so difficult between two people who lack trust or are nursing tensions and resentments.

Yet if trust and closeness are at the heart of what makes sex possible and desirable, this suggests that it must be possible – if conditions required it – to derive the best of sex without actual sex. Were a couple to be highly emotion-ally attuned, were they able to bear their souls and witness each other's deep natures with care and curiosity, were there to be a mutual commitment to tenderness and understand-ing, then it might be possible for them to be as close – and therefore as secure – in each other's platonic arms as a couple that was regularly able to reach orgasm together.

It's by getting more forensic about what is good in sex that one can see how – if circumstances dictated it (distance, illness, bodily incompatibility) – love might endure well enough without any sex at all.

29. You learn that your partner has had a one-night stand. How do you respond?

---

a) End the relationship immediately.

---

b) Try to discover why they are so angry with you.

The most natural and immediate response to learning that a beloved partner has had an affair is to want to end things – indeed, to want to kill them (as they seem, at that moment, to have murdered a part of us). But this response risks cutting us off from an understanding of why an affair happened in the first place – and therefore what, if anything, we might do to repair a frayed bond.

Though society likes to suggest that the chief reason people have affairs is something called 'horniness', in an overwhelming number of cases, what really drives the wish to sleep with a new partner is a feeling of hurt around, and disconnection from, an old one. We aren't so much lustful as alienated and, probably, angry – in ways we're only semiconscious of. An affair is a destructive and inarticulate response to a feeling of disappointment.

If an affair is so unhelpful (quite apart from plain wounding), it is because, in the wake of its discovery, it becomes almost impossible for the betrayed party to be able to take an interest in the nature of their partner's underlying disappointment. They are so beset by their own sense of humiliation, they are so furious and frightened, it is understandably hard for them to wonder what tensions in the relationship might have led to the affair in the first place.

Nevertheless, if curiosity is ever possible, if we can dare to ask 'why?' and listen to the answer with a degree of patience, then the relationship may be salvaged and placed on new foundations. It's by being able to grasp what it was about the existing story that somehow let the partner down, that something may be rescued from the drama. With imagination, we may be able to turn a selfish and inarticulate cry of pain into a set of ideas as to how two people who still care about one another might understand their mutual hurts and relearn to love.

30. What is a successful argument in a couple?

a) When you win.

b) When you both understand why you disagree.

A confusing aspect of relationships is how different the rules of arguments are in them as compared with in the rest of life.

When we enter into an argument with someone, in most situations the goal is simple: we need to win. We need to assault their position with a panoply of superior reasons and points of contention. We need to show them why they cannot have what they want and should probably never have asked for it in the first place.

But, in love, the rules are subtly yet importantly different. When it comes to arguments about where to spend the holidays, how to educate the children or the best way to decorate the living room, the temptation may be to proceed as in a law court and attempt to steamroller our opponent into submission. Yet this is to forget what we are – overall – engaged in in relationships. This is not a forum in which to defeat the other side. As we may need to keep reminding ourselves, we're in fact trying to be close, we're trying to trust, we want an atmosphere of sympathy, we're attempting to love.

Those who are especially good at arguing in life may fail to appreciate a key distinction in relationships: we can either be right, or we can love. We cannot realistically do both. To honour the underlying goal of relationships requires that we undertake a curious exercise: to attempt to understand why our 'opponent' feels as they do, and at the same time to explain – in unaggressive ways – the deeper roots of our contrary opinions, especially as these extend into zones of fear and vulnerability. We need to tell them that their mother scares us with her all-consuming possessiveness – not that we hate her or that they are wrong or idiotic to like her. We need to understand how their taste for bright colours for the living room walls relates to their past – just as they need to hear how our more sober tastes were formed as a response to the pressures of our childhoods. We need, from both sides, to appreciate the reasons for our feelings, instead of being shown with extraordinary linguistic acrobatics precisely how silly and illegitimate they are.

Successful lovers know how much they may need to 'lose' in arguments in order to win at love.

31. Which couple do you think has the highest chances of survival?

a) The one that seems to be always quiet and polite.

b) The one where there are frequent vocal upsets and raised voices.

In the early days of love, we may be understandably wary of arguments. After experiencing tempests in previous relationships, we may delight in calm exchanges with a new partner and an almost magical congruence across a range of areas.

But the very appeal of calm can encourage us to put off, for too long, the requirement to argue when necessary – a pacificism that may endanger the relationship as a whole. Given how obtuse and complicated we all are, we shouldn't imagine any week going by without some degree of resentment building up. It might be over the tardiness with which a partner responded to a request to buy a household item; maybe someone was a bit slow to lend sympathy about an ailment; perhaps there's a feeling in one person that they offer more of the emotional support than the other.

These may be sad realisations, but the place where they belong is out in the open, not in the angry, festering heart of either party. The only way to ensure that complaints don't become grounds for a break-up is to take care that they regularly express themselves as arguments, with raised voices and thunder if necessary. We should, without guilt or reserve, have regular cause to call our partner selfish, to accuse them of missing the point, to point out stupidities and errors – and to have equal accusations thrown back at us.

As psychologists will point out, what dooms couples isn't that they argue; it's that they don't know how to make up. We can have rupture, so long as we know the art of repair: a process that involves extreme efforts to listen, apologise, sympathise, take part of it back and – hopefully – laugh when the heat has begun to ebb. We might argue fifteen times a week if we know how to make up – and still be counted as a good couple. Or, equally, we might argue only once a year and be heading for the end.

We don't – fortunately – need calm in our love stories. We need a capacity to express hurt and listen to complaints with openness; these will always be far greater accomplishments than so-called polite behaviour.

32. How ready might you be – in love – to act the tiny rabbit looking for their 'burrow' (the partner's chest)?

---

a)   What are you talking about?

---

b)   That could be nice.

We call them, for good reason, 'adult' relationships – that is, relationships entered into when we are grown up and committed to the principles and virtues of a mature existence.

What can be paradoxical, therefore, is the extent to which – in the finest couples – the atmosphere owes a debt to certain of the moods and interests of early childhood. For a start, we might want to call the partner 'baby', and they might call us 'poppet'. We might speak in slightly younger voices and in a higher register. We might buy them a furry giraffe and they might buy us an equally adorable soft toy version of a golden retriever. The two animals might even play games with one another and give each other cuddles when they are sad.

It can all look – in the bright light of day – highly unfortunate and regressive. But this would be to overlook how much adult love necessarily sits on a base created in childhood, and therefore should, when it is going well, share certain characteristics with the better moments of our pasts. It is no sign of folly when we use diminutives with our loved ones; it is evidence that we have found our way back to the vulnerability, defencelessness and need that we once knew how to express and entertain with refreshing guilelessness – and that we must reconnect with in order to have a chance to love, even if we are, in the rest of our lives, mature defence attorneys, senior cardiac nurses or lauded venture capitalists.

We might, in turn, wonder at those who appear too keen to dismiss sentimental child-based play as 'babyish'. We might ask what happened to the infantile part of them and why it had to be disowned so forcefully. We might explore how hard it is for them to be witnessed as fragile – and therefore, perhaps, to be gentle around the fragility of others. True maturity doesn't – ultimately – mean quashing all evidence of weakness or immaturity; it means according the younger part of us its due within the totality of our capacities.

We may have to wait until we are real adults before we can relearn how to play – and love – with some of the authenticity and uncensored frankness of our 3-year-old selves.

33. Your partner playfully approaches you one evening and says, in a kindly voice, 'How is my tiny little one today?' How do you feel about this tone?

a) Sick.

b) Touched.

Depending on what happened in our childhoods, going 'back' there – even for a moment, even just for a little game – can prove to be more or less traumatic.

For some of us, the past was such a difficult place that any encounter, however slight, with its atmosphere and dynamics turns out to be repugnant. We don't want to be called small, we don't want to put on funny voices and we don't want to be petted as if we were a sweet 5-year-old. The partner isn't Mummy or Daddy, not even for an instant – and we are not their child. We were probably the sort of people who couldn't wait to grow up, who put away their animals and toys with particular speed and who, in early adolescence, might have taken pride in managing our finances or wearing markedly grown-up clothes.

These are understandable moves, but they may – in subtle ways – militate against true comfort in love, because it's hard to imagine a relationship reaching a truly intimate level without being able to draw upon certain of the modalities of childhood. We might say that a functioning relationship must depend on both parties at points being able to act as Daddy or Mummy to the other's little child (the roles should then be reversed) – an idea that is likely to sicken anyone for whom their original father or mother was hurtful or disappointing.

We all fundamentally long to be grown up and are on the lookout for mature people to connect with. But we can gauge our true level of maturity by asking ourselves how irritated or appalled we might feel if someone called us their little one. True love seems to call for an ability to mother or father the younger self of the partner – and to allow them to do likewise to us.

34. Your partner puts on a 'soppy' movie about a couple who eventually find true love after overcoming many obstacles. How are you tempted to respond to the choice of film?

a) Ridiculous Hollywood nonsense.

b) Idiotic – but adorable.

There's a kind of film that we have all been trained by the guardians of high culture to know is 'bad'. It most likely involves a plot line of absurdly romantic dimensions, in which we are invited to believe in love with special intensity, and to cry about the goodness and eventual happiness of two enticing, star-crossed lovers.

The fear of high-culture guardians is that we might mistake this for real life and that our expectations might be so skewed by the film that we would be unable to navigate the compromises and dullness of more ordinary partners: being moved by the film threatens to open us up to being destroyed by reality.

But it might be possible for us to acknowledge all the flaws in the film as a work of art, to appreciate that it was a far-from-faithful portrayal of relationships, and yet still to discern value in its idealism. Our tears at the fate of the characters would indicate that we willingly maintain – buried beneath all the customary important layers of scepticism and caution – a seam of intense hope as to the prospects of love. And this, far from being dangerous, may turn out to be an important ingredient in ensuring that our relationships have sufficient degrees of thoughtfulness and affection to last the course.

So-called soppiness is not just fragility; it is emblematic of a capacity for soft-heartedness that is required to sweeten the angry and anxious moments of a long-term life with anyone. Someone who knows how to cry at a bad film will probably also be someone who looks after us when we are ill, who sensitively cares about the tears of a child and who would not dismiss us as a loser if we failed. We would be advised to think rather well of tender emotions, and to replenish our own reserves of trust and enthusiasm by surrendering to our share of cinematic tears.

35. Your partner failed to buy you the medicine that you suggested (not very forcefully) they should pick up for you on your way home. How do you respond when you discover this?

---

a) Say nothing, but let them see you buying it for yourself in the morning; they might feel a bit guilty.

---

b) Tell them what they've forgotten and explain that it's upsetting.

There's a general sense at large that 'game-playing' in relationships is a bad thing – and that all good people are opposed to it. 'I don't play games' is a favourite mantra declaimed by hopeful, therapised people at the beginning of love stories the world over.

However, it can be less obvious what game-playing really involves – and therefore how we can definitively avoid its dynamics. We too often associate the sport with its most obvious manifestations in the dating phase: for example, when a person goes cold as soon as love is reciprocated, or stops calling the moment you start to call them.

But there is another form of game-playing within relationships that is far more insidious, invisible and, in the long run, dangerous. It occurs whenever we decide to stop saying something that is on our minds and camouflage an injury instead; when our partner has done or said something that has wounded us, but we choose not to reveal it because to do so would make us feel vulnerable, desperate, cloying and weak before someone who (we fear) might simply not care enough about us to listen. We therefore opt to initiate a so-called game in which we bury our ruffled feelings but do so very badly, in the deliberate hope that our partner will find their offence and then feel sorry for it and apologise – without us having had to be naked about our upset. The 'game' sets out to provoke guilt as an alternative to emotional frankness.

Rather than tell a partner cleanly that we're a bit upset that they didn't buy us the medicine we asked them for, we play the game of blithely not caring. We stay silent and then, the next morning, go to the chemist ourselves and leave the box and the receipt prominently on the kitchen table. When (as we had hoped) they spot it and immediately say, 'Oh god, I'm so sorry,' we smile nonchalantly and reply, 'Don't worry, that's fine, it wasn't a bother for me.'

It may seem like a tiny incident, but the seismologists of relationships will know that this is likely to be the harbinger of something far bigger: a fateful pattern of not declaring what is wrong, of hoping to be read without explaining and of not daring to speak about what matters – all of which can over time lead to a grave erosion of trust and destructive, indirect methods of communication that bring anger and resentment in their wake.

This is normally a strategy that we learnt in childhood around indifferent or temperamental parents – and that we have failed to outgrow.

A true commitment to not playing games involves a profound effort directly to say everything that has upset us on a daily, even hourly, basis. It could sound like we are being 'difficult'. However, so long as we are reasonably polite, communicating hurt is anything but poor behaviour. It's the greatest privilege to be in love with a true adult who can tell us what is amiss precisely when a problem occurs – and is brave enough to present themselves as weak so that love can stay strong.

36. In a train station waiting room, someone else's baby starts to wail and doesn't stop. What do you think?

_____

a) The parent shouldn't give in. If you encourage that kind of behaviour, it'll just keep looking for attention.

_____

b) Poor little thing (but I hope they're not on my train).

Nature has arranged things so that almost no one is able to read a book peacefully while a baby is crying. But the universality of the discomfort provoked by upset babies masks how each one of us interprets the crying deep down. What does the crying mean to us? How do we personally feel about the shrieks? And, in particular, what do we think are the young one's motives?

For one distinctive cohort, the motives are clear: the baby is seeking attention. It is putting on a show. It is trying to get one over on us. It is engaged in a deliberate strategy to annoy us and everyone else in order to get its way. And that's why, once we can be reasonably sure that it isn't actually going to die, the best policy is to ignore the child until it shuts up. To do anything else would be to reward manipulation and generate a lifetime of theatrical tantrums.

Other people, on the other hand, might swiftly assume that something is wrong – even if it's just an upset mind – and will want to lend the baby assistance in whatever way is possible or appropriate.

The difference can – in the end – be explained by our own distinctive histories. It's how we were treated as tiny ones that is likely to determine how we will want to treat other small ones in turn. Our feelings towards the baby are reflections of how others felt about us, and how we now relate to our vulnerable selves.

If this is in any way relevant to love, it's that we will inevitably – at some point in a relationship – encounter the symbolic, child-like wail of our partner. How then will we choose to interpret their pain? Will we see them as an attention-seeking nuisance or give them the benefit of the doubt? Furthermore, how might we relate to the weeping child inside of us? Should it be shut down and told to grow up? Or might it reach out to a partner for reassurance and comfort? Must we be tough people with a cold manner, or can we afford to be tender and affectionate and call for help?

The baby wailing in the waiting room isn't just a nuisance; it's a Rorschach test that shows up how we feel about our and our partner's delicate and dependent needs.

37. At dinner, a prospective partner reveals – with considerable embarrassment – that they have a slightly scarred hand. What do you register?

---

a) An involuntary desire to end the date early.

---

b) An involuntary desire to give them a hug.

We all possess physical features or aspects of our biographies that we feel convinced would disgust a potential partner if they came to know them. It might be bad skin, a setback in our career, an embarrassing relative, a creaking knee. In anxious moments, we are convinced that these problems must deny us a chance at love.

But this is to forget something essential about the spirit of true love: that it isn't merely attracted to strength and perfection; it may collect with particular intensity around vulnerability, weakness and so-called flaws. A scarred hand may prove attractive precisely because it is not like other hands, because it demands special sympathy, because it quietly calls out for kindness and sensitive consideration in a generally heedless and impatient world.

We may not have such a hand ourselves, nor might our partner, but we can understand well enough what this hand symbolises: an aspect of ourselves that we are not proud of, that makes us feel shy and unacceptable. In our earliest years, none of us knew how to be impressive, and yet, if we were lucky, we were loved well enough anyway. We were loved in spite of – or indeed because of – our lisp, our inability to spell and our tendency to spill things down ourselves. From this we know that, however nice it may be to be admired, what we really crave is to be loved for what is less than accomplished about us. We are, by extension, being faithful to the essence of love when we are moved by the less-than-flawless sides of others, when we want to rescue them from shame, when we want to bring their loneliness and self-hatred to an end, when we want to nurse them and attend to their sufferings.

If we are wondering whether someone might be right for us, we may need to ask ourselves only one question: are we principally *impressed* by them or, more importantly (unusual hand or not), *touched* by them?

38. Imagine you have an amazing victory (perhaps at work). How do you feel?

a) Worried.

b) Great.

We can learn a huge amount about ourselves by studying the phenomenon of winning. Ostensibly, winning is something we are all in favour of. We may work long hours in order to win. Victory can be the target of immense efforts and self-discipline across many years; it is hard to imagine that it would bring with it any complications.

And yet when it occurs, it is not always the unambiguous event we might have pictured. How we respond depends, in large part, on how we feel about ourselves. If we are not especially deserving in our own eyes, if we harbour morbid suspicions of our worth, then the moment of victory can provoke an acute sense of being an impostor; we may feel we have somehow cheated and are about to be unmasked or hurt by other people. Winning may be desirable, but it can also be desperately unfamiliar and alarming.

This matters in relationships because contented love is a supreme instance of winning. When we finally find someone we adore and who reciprocates our feelings, we have secured a prize to which we may have aspired throughout our adult lives. However, our most intense impulse may still be to quit the relationship or undermine it in devious ways, not because we actually find fault with our partner, but because we aren't used to the happiness they have brought us.

We become guilty of self-sabotage, whereby we dissolve our happiness on the (unconscious) grounds that we are its unworthy recipients. Our ensuing grief may be painful, but it at least feels more in line with our impression of our due.

One way to loosen this impulse in love is to observe its devilish operations in other areas of our lives, where it may be easier to track and therefore to start to dislodge. We may watch ourselves quitting jobs just after we have been promoted or becoming highly anxious just when we have won the respect of our colleagues or clients.

Our greatest challenge isn't always to find love; it may be to allow ourselves to accept the happiness it threatens to usher in.

39. How do you feel about yourself?

---

a)   I broadly loathe myself.

---

b)   I broadly like myself.

A central question we need to answer when considering our aptness for love is not how we feel about any particular prospective partner; it's how we feel about ourselves.

There can be something unhelpfully familiar in the assertion that we will never be able to love another person if we do not love ourselves – yet the situation is both more nuanced and more awkward than this well-known phrase allows for. It isn't that we can't love when we disdain who we are; it's more precisely that we can't allow ourselves to be loved. So long as we are convinced that we are in essence unworthy, repulsive and suspicious, we will be determined to undermine anyone who seeks to love us. We may love them, but we will apply immense effort to making sure that they end up unable or unwilling to reciprocate.

We may well ask where self-love originates from – and what we might do to correct its shortfalls. How we feel about ourselves is at heart an internalisation of how others close to us – most especially our parents – felt about us during our childhoods. The verdicts of our caregivers shape our eventual judgement of ourselves. Outer voices become inner voices; the admonitions of parental archetypes determine the way one part of us speaks to the other.

Knowing this does not correct the problem at once – but it is the beginning of hope. We can start to see that our relentless self-suspicion doesn't, in reality, owe very much to our character or alleged flaws. Our self-hatred isn't a measured response to who we are. It's something we have uncritically absorbed through the indiscriminate workings of childhood psychology, and we hence retain the right to arrive at a more considered, broad-ranging and imaginative view of our nature. We may not be without error, but we are almost certainly not worthy of the sort of loathing we are used to heaping on ourselves.

When we find ourselves entangled once again in a relationship that seems to be listing in an unfortunate direction, we might address the fate of the uncherished child we once were – for whom contented love may have been longed for yet impossible to accept.

40. How much do you – in areas of life other than love – wonder whether or not you have made the right choice – for example, when choosing a career, a place to live or a new pair of shoes?

a)   I often doubt my choices.

b)   I am generally happy with my choices.

For some of us, the process of settling on a partner is always accompanied by a host of uncomfortable doubts: how can we be sure that we are properly compatible? Are we intellectually well suited? Do our interests align? Are they our type? Might we be able to do better? What if we tire of them? What if they bore us?

These sorts of questions – though they may be understandable on an ad hoc basis – can start to wear away at the legitimacy of any relationship when they become subjects of daily rumination.

Though each question may seem to make surface sense, the business of questioning remorselessly can be a symptom of a deeper – and more unjust – tendency to doubt everything we have chosen, not because there is objectively anything wrong with it, but simply because we have ourselves chosen it. It is in the end really ourselves, not the choice, that we have doubts about – though, to make matters more complicated still, we cannot observe that this is what is at play. Questioning our choices turns out to be yet another subterranean consequence of disliking ourselves.

To determine whether this really is what we are doing, it helps to explore how we feel about our choices in other areas of our lives. How are we around our choice of career? What are we like around our choice of clothes, holiday destinations or restaurant dishes?

This can help us to see that what we may be dealing with is not a particularly doubt-worthy partner, but a tendency in ourselves to doubt anything we have chosen – because we don't trust ourselves to be good judges, or indeed, more broadly and poignantly, good and worthy people. The inability to feel comfortable with our choices is a legacy of a past in which we may have been made to feel severely inadequate around anything we wanted or did.

Our partner may be a very good choice indeed – but if we can never believe that we are capable of making a good choice of any sort, we will never be in a position to appreciate them, however fine they may be. We may need to question the way we feel about our choices in general before we doubt any one choice in particular.

41. How quickly do you conclude that a situation is terrible and doomed: a picnic, a holiday, a work project?

_____

a) Very quickly indeed.

_____

b) Slowly, in general. Things are often fine.

It is a feature of the way our minds work – or don't so much – that we can be well into middle age before we realise some very basic things about ourselves. One of these is the extent to which we may possess what psychologists call a catastrophising mindset.

For the catastrophiser, there is rarely much of a gap between a problem and the onset of what can feel like outright disaster. A wasp has come to disturb us on the deckchair; the holiday is now over. There has been an announcement of a delay to our train; we're going to miss the whole conference. We've hit a difficulty in the third paragraph of a document; the entire report is doomed.

Part of what makes the catastrophiser so jumpy is that they have no clue that this is what they might in fact be. If pushed, they might term themselves 'vigilant', but they don't have any sense that there could be a response other than the melodramatic one they're used to. They don't allow that someone else might react to the arrival of a swarm of wasps by suggesting an afternoon at the museum, or that someone else might think that if the train were severely delayed, we could always take a bus.

Catastrophisers are almost always the children of catastrophisers, the offspring of parents who immediately feared that their little ones would get sunburnt or fall out of the treehouse, destroy their new trousers or fail their exams.

There are always likely to be a few reasons to worry in love: perhaps our partner will look elsewhere, maybe we'll cease to get on so well, one of us might get sick. But resilient people know that there is usually a very large gap between a problem and a calamity, between what might and what generally does happen.

Love may start to feel a lot less dangerous in our eyes when we realise that the whole of our world has, quite unfairly, seemed filled with emergencies and terrors from the start. What we may be dealing with is not so much a very worrying partner as a foreboding-filled mindset we will be in a good position to overcome once we realise it exists.

42. After yet another occasion when they say one thing but then do another, or twist logic in truly odd ways, it dawns on you that your partner may be what is colloquially called a psychopath. You have perhaps already invested a lot in the relationship. What do you do?

---

a) Nothing for a while, then conclude that you might be wrong after all. Surely nothing so strange could be on the cards.

---

b) Leave that day.

The difference between emotionally healthy and unhealthy people does not lie in who they find to date; both parties are likely to end up, at points, in the company of some extremely disturbed candidates. The difference lies in how quickly they manage to spot these figures – and the energy that they can muster to get out.

The most pernicious feature of emotional ill health is that it weakens our ability to parse candidates on the basis of their kindness, goodness or sanity. We can't see who is trouble. A person may come along who says a few sweet things and we are won over. We overlook that they have also asked us for a large loan that they are unlikely ever to be able to pay back. Or that they were fired for bullying a colleague at work or fined for defacing a neighbour's property.

We are so indiscriminate because – usually – we had to make allowances for some impossible people in our own childhoods, at an age when getting away was not an option: we loved a father who beat us up, we explained away the antics of a mother who emotionally neglected us. We expect love to be accompanied by pain. We never learnt the art of protecting ourselves – and of pushing back against cruelty, harmful eccentricity and exploitation. Whatever alarms we have in our minds have all been switched off and their circuits disabled. Someone would more or less have to come at us with a bloodstained knife before we would wake up to an issue.

Healthy people for their part know that a good section of the population is likely to be severely disturbed. They aren't unduly bothered by the statistical chances, but neither do they forget them. And therefore, when they find themselves dating someone who starts to do difficult, uncomfortable things, they have no compunction about calling out the problem – and leaving at the earliest opportunity. Looking after themselves is common sense for them: they've been doing it ever since other people started looking after them well in early childhood.

43. You come to the view that your partner is not, after all, going to be right for you. But by this stage, they are very keen on you and they would be very disappointed – and possibly hysterical with grief – if you called things to an end. What do you do?

---

a) Nothing fast. Letting them down would be too awful. Perhaps wait until the end of the year, or the one after that.

---

b) Tell them right away.

Relationships pose an acute dilemma for those among us who place an immense store on being nice. However well intentioned we may be, however gentle our manner and advanced our ethics, there are likely to be situations in love in which we have no alternative but to make someone very sad. Having brought great happiness to a partner, we may now have to accept that our own growth and contentment will have to rely on breaking their heart. But how, given our tender natures, are we to execute such an 'unkind' manoeuvre? How can we bring ourselves to devastate someone who thinks so well of us?

The temptation is to try to continue to be 'nice' for as long as possible – that is, to say nothing for an age, perhaps until after the trip abroad or their birthday or their parents' anniversary ... It may seem sensitive, but we are – along the way – of course guilty of doing something very mean indeed: encouraging them to place their hopes in a person who has no intention whatsoever of remaining with them; in other words, of wasting their precious life.

So-called nice people (who it turns out can cause an unholy amount of trouble in the world) were not – in their early years – likely to have been privileged enough to have been able to annoy and disappoint people when they needed to. They learnt to tiptoe and dissemble to survive. Behind their timidity lies a fear of an uncontrollable rage or sadness that they might unleash by speaking their truth.

But truly mature and kind people understand that there are moments when niceness is no longer an option, moments when only a degree of brutal frankness can guarantee the welfare of both parties.

When looking for a partner, it is common to look for someone whom we might be with until the end of life. But we should be as careful to try to find (and become) someone with an even more important advantage: the courage and generosity to be able to announce honestly and swiftly when it all deserves to be over.

III.

SCORES & CONCLUSIONS

Having answered forty-three questions, aside from taking a small moment for self-congratulation, it's time to do some counting and award ourselves a score – which will place us into one of three categories.

Every question allows for two answers. The first, labelled a), is the problematic one; it indicates a response that may be unhelpful to the development of love. The second, labelled b), indicates maturity and an advanced capacity for connection.

— Every a) answer should be assigned 1.
— Every b) answer should be assigned 5.

The total should then be added to identify which category we are in.

(i)   161–215: Mature and ready for love

We are ready to succeed at love partly because we don't expect things to be easy. We understand the degree of effort that is to be expected in any fulfilling union. We are not waiting for magical enchantment: we know that we and even the best partner are only ever flawed humans. At the same time, we retain a healthy degree of idealism; experience has not rendered us bitter or defensive. We can still be thrilled; love is hard but not impossible. Around partners, we can communicate our desires and upsets; we do not expect them to understand us wordlessly. We can speak our needs without shame and thereby ensure that our boundaries are known and observed. We appreciate how to compromise. We are less interested in being right than in being close; what interests us is to understand another's mind and to guide them around our psyches in turn. We know the risks of intimacy and are prepared to take them on; there's no point being in a relationship if we can't make ourselves vulnerable. Our love lives may not always go well. We can never be entirely protected from the eccentric or damaging figures we may cross paths with, but our minds are likely to alert us to problems soon enough – and to lend us the confidence to make a new start. Most of all, we are able to tolerate being alone – which guarantees us the inner freedom to wait as long as may be necessary to find the sort of partner we can respect and adore. We may not have found happiness in love yet, but the chances that we will one day are high.

(ii)   81–160: Almost ready for love

We have not come through our pasts unscathed. We are prone to a number of dynamics that can make us difficult to be around – even if we will, in our more self-righteous moods, deny that we are any such a thing. Love presents terrors. It asks us to depend wholeheartedly on someone we can never control; it lays us open to being objects of judgement; we can never be sure that we will be properly understood or cherished as we long to be; we may be abandoned. This asks a lot of us: we can get very frightened indeed of being left. No wonder that we may affect an offhand manner to protect us from the difficulties of dependence, or that we sometimes ask for excessive reassurance. We may not be used to communicating who we are directly; we have had to hide a lot of ourselves from people who didn't have our best interests at heart. It is hard to believe that we could be both honest and tolerated. Still, there are plenty of grounds for hope. We are doing a questionnaire like this for a start. We are committed to psychological exploration and growth. We can have a sense of humour about our follies. We recognise that we are a bit 'mad', but we have the confidence to accept that everyone else is too, and that the best form of maturity we are all capable of is one in which we can admit to our eccentricities and greet news of those of others with benevolence and sympathy. We will never enjoy perfect love, but things may well – in time – come to feel very much 'good enough'.

(iii)   80 and below: A way to go until successful love

We probably aren't too surprised to find ourselves in this category. We've known love to be difficult from the start. It isn't that we necessarily find it hard to get into relationships; we're just experts at getting into the wrong ones, at alienating those we care for, at ending up in repetitive arguments or at being unable to disentangle ourselves from partners as soon as we realise they are harming us. We can hazard one overarching supposition: that we were almost certainly not loved properly in our young years. More than we can sometimes bear to accept, our patterns of love are determined in our childhoods and, for us, this period was arduous. The precise details will vary, but we can surmise that there will have been neglect, a sense of never having been good enough and a lack of role models that could inspire faith in the possibilities of kindness and reliability. We are both cynical and naïve. We long for love just as much as anyone else; it's just that we need to work far harder than others to overcome certain inner obstacles to being able to locate and enjoy it. We need to imagine that some people can be trusted (after we have done some due diligence), that we can be rewarded for honesty and that we do not have to be embarrassed by our desires. There is no need for despair. The goal here isn't total sanity or normality, but a willingness to accept that we may not be quite ready for love as we are right now, which can spur us onto new journeys of discovery and repair.

We may be in the bottom stream, but there are possibilities for progression and every chance of an eventual contented graduation and destiny.

We might propose that – beneath all our considerations of love – lie six essential components of emotional maturity that belie any successful relationship. There are so many ways in which to undermine love; these six qualities amount to a checklist of requirements for romantic redemption and fulfilment.

1. Self-love

We have to begin with ourselves and unpeel the layers of self-suspicion our past may have coated us with. We are not – whatever our instincts tell us – despicable. We aren't worthy of being ignored or taunted. We can dare to receive kindness and allow someone else to be more generous to us than we have ever been to ourselves.

2. Self-exploration

It can feel deeply frightening to enter certain rooms of our minds. But until we do so, we won't be able to stop acting out the dynamics of our tortured pasts. We must accept that we are the products of our histories and develop the strength to explore our sadness and our losses. We should make friends with psychotherapy and the emotional understanding it stands for.

3. Boundaries

We should acknowledge how much we may have grown inclined to let others demean and ignore us. We may have made some unfortunate choices for a stubborn reason: because it feels so much more normal to be treated badly.

4. Suspicion of instinct

We should realise that most of our instincts are wrong. Those we immediately love and those we're immediately bored by aren't necessarily who we think they are. It is perhaps fair enough for many people to follow their gut, but our gut has had trouble knowing what is what for a while. We have no choice but to attempt assiduously to run matters through reason. 'Go with your feelings' is not a well-meaning phrase we should ever listen to.

5. Honesty

Our every impulse in love may be to lie: about how we feel, what we want and who we are. We may have had no native experience of speaking the truth and of things turning out well. But we cannot love until we accede to more direct methods of communication. We have to take the gamble that we could be known, speak, complain – and still be loved.

6. Vulnerability

We may have tried hard to protect ourselves completely – including not loving at all, loving unavailable people and staying in relationships we knew would fail. But we have to take on the risk of opening up if we're to have any chance at true love. Vulnerability doesn't have to be as frightening as it once was. We're capable and strong people now; we've got through a lot and could survive worse. Love is a gamble worth taking.

With such tenets in mind, we should feel free to approach the sorrows and joys of love with confidence and measured excitement, wryly amused by the glorious human comedy we have the privilege to partake in for many more tumultuous and thrilling years yet.

Also available from The School of Life:

How to Find Love

**A guide to navigating the emotional minefield
of love and relationships.**

Choosing a partner is one of the most consequential and tricky decisions we will ever make, and the cost of repeated failure is immense.

How to Find Love explains why we have the 'types' we do, and how our early experiences give us scripts of how and whom we love. It sheds light on harmful repetitive patterns and the extent to which we are not always simply choosing people who can make us happy. We learn the most common techniques we use to sabotage our chances of fulfilment and why, despite their costs, we unwittingly engage in them.

The book provides a crucial set of ideas to help us make safer, more imaginative and more effective choices in love.

ISBN: 978-0-9955736-9-7

Why You Will Marry the Wrong Person

A pessimist's guide to marriage; offering insight, practical advice and consolation.

We are all desperate, of course, to marry the right person. But none of us ever quite does. The fault isn't entirely our own; it has to do with the devilish truth that anyone we're liable to meet is going to be rather wrong, in some fascinating way or another, because this is simply what all humans happen to be – including, sadly, ourselves.

Yet – as these darkly encouraging and witty essays propose – we don't need perfection to be happy. So long as we enter our relationships in the right spirit, we have every chance of coping well enough with, and even delighting in, the inevitable and distinctive wrongness that lies in ourselves and our beloveds.

ISBN: 978-0-9955736-2-8

The School of Life: Quotes to Live By

A collection to revive and inspire

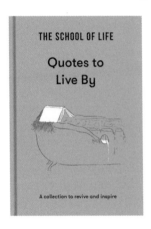

**A collection of enlightening quotes to deliver some
of the most important lessons The School of Life has to offer,
accompanied by humorous illustrations.**

This is a selection of the very best and most psychologically acute quotations from The School of Life, covering such large and diverse topics as relationships, regret, anxiety, work, friends, family, travel and, not least, the meaning of life. Some of these quotations elicit an immediate nod of recognition, others leave us thoughtful – and a few are just plain funny.

Together, this collection of quotations amounts to a tour around the most profound sorrows and joys of the human mind and heart – in a compact format ideally suited to our impatient, anxious, searching times.

ISBN: 978-1-915087-04-1

The Couple's Workbook

Homework to help love last

Therapeutic exercises to help couples nurture patience, forgiveness and humour.

Love is a skill, not just an emotion – and in order for us to get good at it, we have to practise, as we would in any other area we want to shine in.

Here is a workbook containing the very best exercises that any couple can undertake to help their relationship function optimally – exercises to foster understanding, patience, forgiveness, humour and resilience in the face of the many hurdles that invariably arise when you try to live with someone else for the long term.

The notion of exercising is well understood in many areas; we should grant that it applies equally to love. No one can be intuitively good at relationships. We all need to do some homework to become the best partners and couples we can be.

ISBN: 978-1-912891-26-9

The School of Life publishes a range of books on essential topics in psychological and emotional life, including relationships, parenting, friendship, careers and fulfilment. The aim is always to help us to understand ourselves better – and thereby to grow calmer, less confused and more purposeful. Discover our full range of titles, including books for children, here:

www.theschooloflife.com/books

The School of Life also offers a comprehensive therapy service, which complements, and draws upon, our published works:

www.theschooloflife.com/therapy